I am Hindu

Cath Senker
Photography by Jenny Matthews

W

© 2005 Franklin Watts

First published in 2005
by Franklin Watts
96 Leonard Street
London
EC2A 4XD

Franklin Watts Australia
45-51 Huntley Street
Alexandria
NSW 2015

Acknowledgements
The author and publishers would like to thank the following for all their help
in the production of this book: Nimish, Anita, Janaki, Jasmine and Nikhil
Desai, Sita and Gopi Patel, Rasamandala Das, Shruti Dharma Prabhu.

The photos on pages 9, 10, 23b, 26 and 27 were kindly provided
by the Desai family.

Photographer Jenny Matthews
Designer Steve Prosser
Series editor Adrian Cole
Art Director Jonathan Hair
Consultant Rasamandala Das,
ISKCON Educational Services

ISBN 0 7496 5930 0

Dewey Classification 294.5

A CIP catalogue record for this book is available from the British Library.

Printed in China

Contents

All about me

Here I am playing the tabla — Indian drums.

My name's Jasmine Devaki Desai and I'm nine. I like riding my bike with my friends and playing with my cousins.

At school I enjoy history and art, and playing football at break time.

I'm lucky to have cousins that live nearby.

I have an African Grey parrot called Rani.
Having a pet helps me learn to love animals.

My family

Our family, with my uncle and several of my cousins. We're a close family.

I live in Oxford with my mum, dad, brother and sister. My sister Janaki is ten and my brother Nikhil is four. My dad's an optician. Mum looks after us and our home.

Dad was born in England and Mum was born in Kenya, East Africa. Both their families originally came from India.

'It was so exciting to visit India for the first time. We saw the Taj Mahal.' Janaki

Our Hindu beliefs

Hindus believe there is one caring
and loving God who has many forms.

Some of the forms
of God (from lower
left to right):
Hanuman, Lakshman,
Rama and Sita.

We believe that we have
many lives. If we are good in this life
we will have a good life next time.

I think we should be kind and help people around us and in poor countries. It is wrong to fight wars.

Cows are **sacred** to us.
There are cows at our **mandir.**

Worship at home

We have our own **shrine** at home.
In the morning, after our bath, we pray there.

This is our home shrine, where we pray and make **offerings.**

We wake the **deities** with songs and offerings. To show respect, we fan them and bow down to them.

In our kind of Hinduism, the main forms of God we worship are Radha and Krishna.

I make an offering of incense at our shrine.

Our food

I'm a vegetarian, so I eat no meat, fish or eggs. My family doesn't eat **ghee** for health reasons.

I like helping Mum to make chapatis (Indian flat bread).

On fast days (twice a month) we avoid food with rice, grains, flour, lentils and some spices.

We often eat vegetable curry with chapatis and salad. I love nachos and vegetable lasagne, too.

In our holy book, the **Bhagavad Gita**, it says that we should offer food to Krishna before we eat it.

I help to serve chapatis at the mandir.

Our clothes

I normally wear English clothes, but when we go to the mandir I love dressing in my Indian outfits.

I wear an embroidered top with matching trousers, and bangles. Mum wears her sari.

At the mandir the **priest** places a **tilak** mark on my forehead. It shows I'm a follower of Krishna.

The tilak mark means my body is God's temple and I must look after it.

Going to the mandir

On Sunday we go to the Manor, a beautiful mandir in the countryside. There we worship Krishna.

I ring the bell to tell the deities I have come to pray.

During worship, we face the shrine and **chant** to Krishna.

We bow down in front of the deities to show respect.

The priest performs the **arti** ceremony and makes offerings to the deities. Then we listen to a reading from the Bhagavad Gita.

The priest offers fire to the deities and it becomes sacred. We receive blessings from it.

Our holy books

We have many holy books. The Bhagavad Gita is important. There are also beautiful Hindu stories.

The Ramayana is a story that tells how good wins over evil.

We have story books about Krishna's life.

My favourite story is about Sudama Brahmin, a poor priest. He visited his friend Krishna, but could only offer a simple rice dish. Krishna accepted the gift happily and turned the man's small hut into a palace.

The Hindu priest

A Hindu priest leads worship in the mandir. He is the only one allowed into the shrine room to care for the deities. Each day he washes them, dresses them and makes offerings of food.

'The priest explains the meaning of our customs in a clear, simple way.' Jasmine's dad.

The priest makes a tilak mark on my forehead.

The priest marries couples, blesses newborn babies and recites **mantras** (prayers) when a person dies.

A priest married my mum and dad.

Learning about my religion

I mostly learn about Hinduism from my parents. At my Gujarati class I learn my family's Indian language and study our religion, too.

I've learnt the Gujarati alphabet.

At my dance class we learn traditional Indian dancing. This year we performed at the Oxford carnival in front of lots of people. Our dance showed how God created the world.

Janaki and I learn special movements for our dance.

My favourite festival

My favourite festival is Janmashtami, Krishna's birthday. At the mandir, we fast until midnight, the time of his birth. We listen to stories about Krishna and watch a puppet show.

We take it in turns to rock an image of baby Krishna on a swing.

I love drama. **T**his year I was in a play about Krishna at the festival.

At midnight, the priest performs arti. After offering prayers and presents to Krishna, we eat his favourite dishes - delicious foods made with milk and butter.

Many dancers perform at the festival, too.

Glossary

arti
Moving lighted candles in a circle to show respect to the forms of God on the shrine.

Bhagavad Gita
One of the most important Hindu holy books.

chant
A prayer with a few words that are sung repeatedly.

deity
A form of God.

ghee
An oil made from butter, which is often used in Indian cooking.

incense
A stick that is burned to give off a nice smell.

mandir
The Hindu place of worship, sometimes called a temple.

mantra
A sacred sound or word that is usually said again and again. Mantras are important in many Hindu ceremonies.

offerings
Things that are offered to the deities on the shrine.

priest
A person who performs religious duties in the temple.

sacred
Connected with God; holy.

shrine
A place, sometimes at home, where people worship.

tilak
A mark worn by Hindus on the forehead. It is made from a special paste and varies depending on the way the person follows Hinduism.

Websites

http://atschool.eduweb.co.uk/manorlh/hinduism/hindui.html
Information for primary school children about Hindu gods and goddesses, worship, holy books, sacred symbols, stories and festivals.

www.bbc.co.uk/religion/religions/hinduism/
All about Hindu history, customs, beliefs, worship and holy days.

www.btinternet.com/~vivekananda/schoolsl.htm
Hinduism for schools site with pages on God, rebirth, worship, prayers and scriptures (including the Bhagavad Gita).

http://hinduism.about.com/od/hinduismforkids/
A page with links to sites with resources about Hinduism for children of all ages.

www.hindukids.org/index.html
Includes pages and activities about Hindu prayer, greetings, stories and festivals.

www.krishnatemple.com/manor/manor.shtm
Adult site about Bhaktivedanta Manor, where Jasmine and her family worship.

Note to parents and teachers
Every effort has been made by the Publishers to ensure that these websites are suitable for children; that they are of the highest educational value, and that they contain no inappropriate or offensive material. However, because of the nature of the Internet, it is impossible to guarantee that the contents of these sites will not be altered. We strongly advise that Internet access is supervised by a responsible adult.

Index